EXPLORE THE U.S.A.

NEBRASKA

Megan Kopp

LET'S READ

AV2 BY WEIGL

ADDED VALUE • AUDIO VISUAL

W9-APJ-378

LET'S READ
AV2
BY WEIGL™
ADDED VALUE • AUDIO VISUAL

Go to **www.av2books.com**, and enter this book's unique code.

BOOK CODE

D 4 8 4 4 4 6

AV² by Weigl brings you media enhanced books that support active learning.

AV² provides enriched content that supplements and complements this book. Weigl's AV² books strive to create inspired learning and engage young minds in a total learning experience.

Your AV² Media Enhanced books come alive with...

Audio
Listen to sections of the book read aloud.

Video
Watch informative video clips.

Embedded Weblinks
Gain additional information for research.

Try This!
Complete activities and hands-on experiments.

Key Words
Study vocabulary, and complete a matching word activity.

Quizzes
Test your knowledge.

Slide Show
View images and captions, and prepare a presentation.

... and much, much more!

Published by AV² by Weigl
350 5th Avenue, 59th Floor
New York, NY 10118
Website: www.av2books.com   www.weigl.com

Library of Congress Cataloging-in-Publication Data

Kopp, Megan.
 Nebraska / Megan Kopp.
   p. cm. -- (Explore the U.S.A.)
Includes bibliographical references and index.
ISBN 978-1-61913-373-0 (hard cover : alk. paper)
1. Nebraska--Juvenile literature. I. Title.
F666.3.K67 2013
978.2--dc23
                        2012015605

Printed in the United States of America in North Mankato, Minnesota
1 2 3 4 5 6 7 8 9 16 15 14 13 12

052012
WEP040512

Project Coordinator: Karen Durrie
Art Director: Terry Paulhus

Weigl acknowledges Getty Images as the primary image supplier for this title.

NEBRASKA

Contents

3

This is Nebraska.
It is called the Cornhusker State.
Nebraska is known for its corn.

6

This is the shape of Nebraska. It is in the middle of the United States.

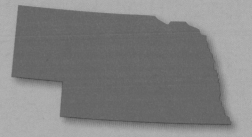

Where is Nebraska?

N
W · E
S

Canada

Pacific Ocean

United States

Atlantic Ocean

Mexico

Nebraska shares a border with six other states.

Settlers began farming in Nebraska in the middle of the 1800s. It became part of the United States in 1867.

People were given free land to start farms in the 1860s.

The goldenrod is the Nebraska state flower. It can grow up to 4 feet high.

Nebraska's state seal shows a river, a steamboat, and a train.

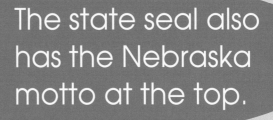

The state seal also has the Nebraska motto at the top.

This is the state flag of Nebraska. It has the gold and silver state seal on a blue background.

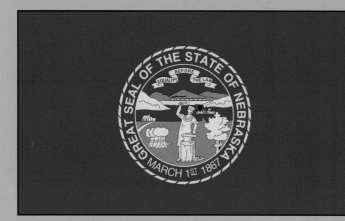

Nebraska was one of the last states to choose an official flag.

The state animal of Nebraska is the white-tailed deer. It is named for the white fur under its tail. White-tailed deer can weigh up to 350 pounds.

Male white-tailed deer grow large antlers.

Lincoln is the capital of Nebraska. It started as a small farming town in 1856.

The tower at the capitol building is 400 feet high.

Many farmers grow corn in Nebraska. Farmers also grow soybeans, hay, and wheat. Farms cover most of the land in Nebraska.

Nebraska also has many cattle ranches.

Nebraska is known for its beautiful rivers.

Some people visit Nebraska to paddle boats down the Missouri River. Others come to learn about the history of Nebraska.

NEBRASKA FACTS

These pages provide detailed information that expands on the interesting facts found in the book. These pages are intended to be used by adults as a learning support to help young readers round out their knowledge of each state in the *Explore the U.S.A.* series.

Pages 4–5

Nebraska is called the Cornhusker State after its main crop. This name comes from the method of harvesting, or "husking," corn by hand, which was common in Nebraska before the invention of husking machinery. Nebraska has also been called the Tree Planter's State. Only two percent of Nebraska is naturally forested. Nebraska was the first state to celebrate Arbor Day.

Pages 6–7

On March 1, 1867, Nebraska became the 37th state to join the United States. The wide open prairies and rolling plains of Nebraska lie halfway between the Atlantic and Pacific Oceans. Nebraska is bordered by six other states. South Dakota is to the north, Iowa and Missouri are to the east, Kansas lies to the south, and Colorado and Wyoming are to the west.

Pages 8–9

American Indians have lived in the Nebraska area for about 10,000 years. The first recorded European in Nebraska was a French explorer who built a trading post on the Platte River in 1714. In the mid-1800s, thousands of pioneers crossed through Nebraska on the Oregon Trail. The Homestead Act of 1862 granted 160 acres (65 hectares) of land to any settler who farmed it.

Pages 10–11

Goldenrod flowers are bright yellow and can grow up to 4 feet (1.2 meters) high. Goldenrod leaves can be used to make tea and medicine. The state seal shows a steamboat on the Missouri River, which runs along Nebraska's northern and eastern borders. The steamboat and train represent the transportation of Nebraska's crops to the rest of the country. The state motto, "Equality Before the Law," means the law protects all people equally.

Pages 12–13

The Nebraska flag shows the state seal in gold and silver on a blue background. The mountains and river on the state seal show the land's natural riches. The wheat and settler's cabin represent agriculture, and the blacksmith symbolizes industry. Nebraska's state motto is on a ribbon at the top of the seal. The flag was adopted in 1925.

Pages 14–15

The white-tailed deer is Nebraska's state animal. This deer has reddish-brown fur during summer, but it turns grayish-brown in winter. Male deer, called bucks, have antlers during summer and fall months. When it senses danger, the white-tailed deer lifts its tail to display the white fur underneath.

Pages 16–17

Lincoln was founded as a farming community in 1856. The city became the state capital in 1867. Lincoln now has a population of more than 250,000. It is the second-largest city in the state, after Omaha. Nebraska's capitol was completed in 1933. The tower is 400 feet (122 m) high and can be seen from miles (km) around.

Pages 18–19

About 93 percent of Nebraska's land is used for agricultural purposes, such as farming and ranching. Good soil for farmland has become one of Nebraska's most valuable resources. Irrigation is important in the warm, dry summer months. Nebraska is a leading corn producer. Its annual corn crop is the third-largest of any state in the country.

Pages 20–21

People come to Nebraska for its many outdoor activities and historic sites. Visitors can paddle along the Lewis and Clark Expedition route on the Missouri River. At Scotts Bluff National Monument, summertime visitors can relive life on the Oregon Trail. Nebraska is also known for its rodeos. The state's first rodeo was put on in the 1880s by Buffalo Bill Cody, one of the best-known cowboys of the Old West.

KEY WORDS

Research has shown that as much as 65 percent of all written material published in English is made up of 300 words. These 300 words cannot be taught using pictures or learned by sounding them out. They must be recognized by sight. This book contains 52 common sight words to help young readers improve their reading fluency and comprehension. This book also teaches young readers several important content words, such as proper nouns. These words are paired with pictures to aid in learning and improve understanding.

Page	Sight Words First Appearance
4	for, is, it, its, state, the, this
7	a, in, of, other, where, with
8	began, farms, given, land, part, people, start, to, were
11	also, and, at, can, feet, grow, has, high, river, shows, up
12	an, last, on, one, was
15	animal, large, named, under, white
16	as, small
19	many, most
20	about, come, down, learn, some

Page	Content Words First Appearance
4	corn, cornhusker, Nebraska
7	border, middle, shape, United States
8	settlers
11	flower, goldenrod, motto, seal, steamboat, top, train
12	background, flag
15	antlers, fur, pounds, tail, white-tailed deer
16	capital, capitol building, Lincoln, tower, town
19	hay, cattle ranches, soybeans, wheat
20	boats, history, Missouri River